Kent,

Learning how to be kind to others

Learning How to Be Kind to Others

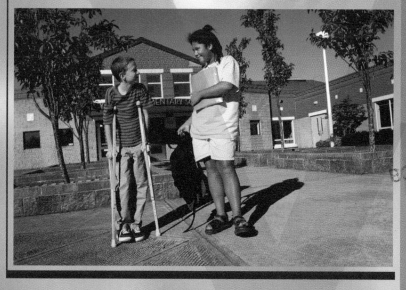

Susan Kent

The Rosen Publishing Group's
PowerKids Press™
New York

For Olga Melbardis and George Badenoch, exemplars of
kindness—to me and everyone.

Published in 2001 by The Rosen Publishing Group, Inc.
29 East 21st Street, New York, NY 10010

First Edition

Book Design: Maria E. Melendez

Photo Credits: Cover and title page, pp. 7, 8, 11, 15, 16, 19, 20 by Debra Rothstein-Brewer;
pp. 4, 12 © Skjold Photographs.

Kent, Susan, 1942–
    Learning how to be kind to others/ by Susan Kent.
       p. cm.— (The violence prevention library)
    Includes index.
    Summary: Explains why it is important to be kind to family, friends, and acquaintances and
shows different ways to be kind.
    ISBN 0-8239-5613-X (lib. bdg.: alk. paper)
    1. Kindness—Juvenile literature. [1. Kindness.] I. Title. II. Series.
BJ1533.K5 K46 2000
177'.7—dc21   99-054582

Manufactured in the United States of America

Contents

When People Are Mean to Us

We all know how bad it feels when people are mean to us. However, we do not always think about how they might feel if we are not nice to them. You would probably feel sad and left out if you were not invited to a friend's birthday party, but maybe you have not invited that friend to your house to play in a long time.

If you want other people to be kind to you, you should first think about how to be kind to them. If you treat other people well, maybe they will do the same for you.

◀ *It feels bad when people are mean to you.*

Being Polite Shows Respect

One of the easiest ways to treat people well is to be **polite**. Always remember to say "please" and "thank you." At school you can welcome new classmates and introduce them to your friends. If you see someone fall on the stairs, don't laugh. Help that person up and ask if you can do anything else to help. When a friend wins first prize at the science fair, say, "Great job!" You would want your classmates to do the same for you. Politeness is a way of being kind. Being polite shows **respect** for everyone.

Helping someone get up when he or she falls is one way of being polite. ▶

Kindness at Home

At home our families are often kind to us. Sometimes, though, they are not. When Jake's parents are tired and cranky after a long day at work, they sometimes yell at him even though he hasn't done anything wrong.

We want our families to be kind to us, but we do not always think about being nice to them. If you try to be kind to your family members, you might be able to make your home a happier place. When you notice your parents are tired, instead of asking them to do something for you, ask what you can do to help them.

You can be kind and helpful by lending a hand when it is time to set the table.

Serita and Lisa

Serita thought her younger sister Lisa was a real pest. She did not want to play with her. One day she watched Lisa having fun playing dodgeball with her friends. A new girl joined the game and started teasing Lisa for being so skinny. The new girl pushed Lisa right out of the game. Serita thought about how mean this girl was to Lisa, and she felt **ashamed** of how mean she had been to her sister. The next day, she asked Lisa to ride bikes with her. The sisters had a lot of fun together. In time they became great friends.

Spend time with your brothers or sisters. You may turn out to be great friends. ▶

Friends Are Kind to Each Other

It is usually easy to be kind to friends. You spend time together and listen to each other. If a friend asks you for help, you are probably glad to give it. Helping friends often feels like fun.

It is also important, though, to be kind to friends when it is not easy. For example, if a friend gets the part in a play that you wanted, you might feel upset. It may take an extra effort to be kind. Try to praise your friends when they are successful instead of feeling **envious**. This is a good way to stay friends with the people you care about.

Praise your friends when they do a good job or when you have all done a good job together.

Kindness at School

You spend a lot of time at school, so don't forget to be kind there, too. You can start in the classroom by showing **consideration** to your teacher and classmates. It is polite to listen, instead of talking, when your teacher explains a lesson. You learn more, too. You and your classmates might also offer to help pass out papers or erase the chalkboard.

Your kindness will be appreciated by everyone and will make your classroom a better place for you, your teacher, and your classmates.

You can be helpful in school by passing out papers to your classmates. ▶

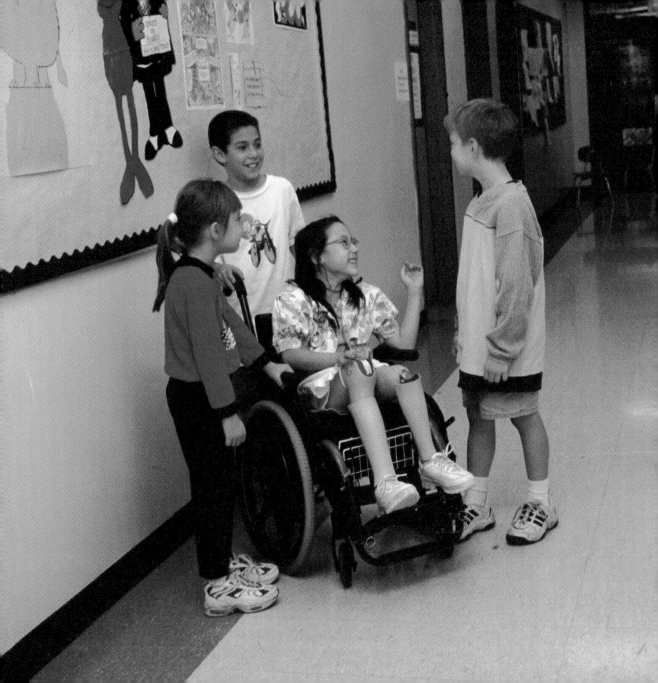

Showing Kindness to Classmates

It is also very important to be kind to your classmates. Be sure to treat everyone politely and with respect. **Compliment** your classmates on their projects or on a good grade. Cheer for athletes and those who perform on stage. Speak up for classmates who are being teased. Appreciate the differences in people. Try to find a way to include anyone who is being left out. When classmates show this kind of consideration for each other, school is a happier place for everyone.

◀ *Sometimes people's differences make friendships more fun and interesting.*

Kindness and Tolerance

Everyone wants to fit in at school and have friends. Some students try to do this by joining a group. If you are part of a group at school, be sure it doesn't turn into a **clique** that **excludes** others. If you ever feel pressure from your group to be mean to someone who is different, remember how you feel when people are mean to you. Stand up to your group and show **tolerance** and kindness to others. You will feel better about yourself if you do. You will feel strong and **confident**. Others will notice your kindness and will want to be your friend.

Take time to learn about people's interests. It can be a lot of fun. ▶

Greg and Andy

Greg is popular at school. He is good at sports and at making up funny stories. Lots of kids want to sit with him at lunch. Greg notices that Andy usually sits alone at lunch. He goes over to Andy's table to eat with him. Greg asks Andy questions about his hobbies and favorite sports to make sure he joins in the **conversation**. When he learns that Andy likes to draw cartoons, they plan to make a comic book together. Greg's kindness leads to a new friendship.

◀ *Greg and Andy are having fun getting to know one another.*

Being Kind Everywhere

School and home are not the only places you can make better by being kind. You will find you have a more pleasant life if you are kind to people wherever you go. When you are polite to salesclerks, you get better help. When you give your bus seat to an older person or help someone cross the street, you are doing a deed that makes both of you feel good.

Kindness will not solve all of your problems. You may be surprised, though, at how much it helps make your world a happier place.

Glossary

ashamed (uh-SHAYMD) To feel uncomfortable because you have done something wrong.

clique (KLIK) A group of friends that doesn't include others in its activities.

compliment (KAHM-pluh-ment) Something good that has been said about you.

confident (KON-fih-dent) Believing in yourself.

consideration (kon-sid-er-AY-shun) Careful thought.

conversation (con-ver-SAY-shun) When people talk to each other.

excludes (eks-KLOODZ) To keep someone out of a group or activity.

envious (EN-vee-us) To want what someone else has.

polite (puh-LYT) To behave well in front of others.

respect (ree-SPEKT) To think highly of someone or something.

tolerance (TAH-ler-ens) Acceptance of people's differences.

Index

24